improving
your
parenting

homebuilders
PARENTING SERIES®

improving
your
parenting

by
dennis & barbara
rainey

FAMILYLIFE®
Little Rock, Arkansas

IMPROVING YOUR PARENTING
FamilyLife Publishing®
5800 Ranch Drive
Little Rock, Arkansas 72223
1-800-FL-TODAY • FamilyLife.com

FLTI, d/b/a FamilyLife®, is a ministry of Campus Crusade for Christ International®

Unless otherwise noted, Scripture quotations are from the Holy Bible, English Standard Version, copyright © 2001 by Crossway Bibles, a division of Good News Publishers. Used by permission. All rights reserved.

ISBN: 978-1-60200-352-1

The HomeBuilders Parenting Series® is a registered trademark of FLTI, d/b/a FamilyLife.

Design: Brand Navigation, LLC

Cover image: © iStockphoto.com/Grady Reese Photography

Printed in the United States of America

16 15 14 13 12   2 3 4 5 6

Unless the Lᴏʀᴅ builds the house,
those who build it labor in vain.

Pꜱᴀʟᴍ 127:1

welcome to homebuilders

When we bring a new life into the world, we burst with pride and joy... but are often unprepared to raise that child to become a mature, responsible adult.

In response to this need, FamilyLife has developed the HomeBuilders Parenting Series with several goals in mind: (1) to encourage you and help you not to feel overwhelmed by the responsibilities of parenting, (2) to help you develop a practical and biblical plan for parenting, (3) to enhance and strengthen your teamwork as a couple, (4) to help you connect with other parents so you can encourage and help one another, and (5) to help you strengthen your relationship with God.

You will notice as you proceed through this study that the Bible is cited as the authority on issues of life, marriage, and parenting. The Bible is God's Word—His blueprint for building a godly home and for dealing with the practical issues of living. Although written nearly two thousand years ago, Scripture still speaks clearly and powerfully about the concerns we face in our families.

A Special Word to Single Parents

Although the primary audience for this study is married couples, we recognize that single parents can also benefit from the experience. If you are a single parent, you will find that while some of the language may not be directed to your circumstances, the teaching and principles are highly applicable and can help you develop a solid, workable plan for your family.

Do we really need to be part of a group? Couldn't we just go through this study as a couple?

While you could work through the study as a couple, you would miss the opportunity to connect with friends and to learn from one another's experiences. You will find that the questions in each session not only help you grow closer to your spouse, but they also create an environment of warmth and fellowship with other couples as you study together.

What does it take to lead a HomeBuilders group?

Leading a group is much easier than you may think, because the leader is simply a facilitator who guides the participants through the discussion questions. You are not teaching the material but are helping the couples discover and apply biblical truths. The special dynamic of a HomeBuilders group is that couples teach themselves.

The study guide you're holding has all the information and guidance you need to participate in or lead a HomeBuilders group. You'll find leader's notes in the back of the guide, and additional helps are posted online at FamilyLife.com/Resources.

What is the typical schedule?

Most studies in the HomeBuilders Parenting Series are six to eight weeks long, indicated by the number of sessions in the guide. The sessions are designed to take sixty minutes in the group with a project for the couples to complete between sessions.

Isn't it risky to talk about your family in a group?

The group setting should be enjoyable and informative—and nonthreatening. **THREE SIMPLE GROUND RULES** will help ensure that everyone feels comfortable and gets the most out of the experience:

1. Share nothing that will embarrass your spouse or violate the trust of your children.
2. You may pass on any question you do not want to answer.
3. If possible, as a couple complete the HomeBuilders project between group sessions.

What other help does FamilyLife offer?

Our list of marriage and family resources continues to grow. Visit FamilyLife.com to learn more about our:

- Weekend to Remember® getaway, The Art of Marriage®, and other events;
- slate of radio broadcasts, including the nationally syndicated *FamilyLife Today*®, *Real FamilyLife*® *with Dennis Rainey*, and *FamilyLife This Week*®;
- multimedia resources for small groups, churches, and community networking;
- interactive products for parents, couples, small-group leaders, and one-to-one mentors; and
- assortment of blogs, forums, and other online connections.

on improving your parenting

Of all the jobs you'll have in your lifetime, none will be more rewarding than parenting. Or more challenging. As your children grow each day—getting bigger physically, developing their unique personalities, and inching toward independence—you'll be their teacher, counselor, disciplinarian, intercessor, coach, cheerleader, and much more.

Think about it: That young life you're shaping will be an adult not many years from now. He'll likely be a husband and father, or she'll be a wife and mother. And they'll approach life in much the same way that they experienced it in their childhoods when you were raising them. Your influence will flow into the next generation and the next. And beyond.

Feeling as though you could use some help?

As parents, we all feel that way sometimes. And we're right: we do need help. Obviously God thinks so; He's devoted much of His written Word, the Bible, to instructing parents how to raise our children and warning us what could happen if we neglect our responsibility.

Improving Your Parenting covers some of the issues that parents have asked most about over the years. We trust that you and your friends will find this study helpful, and that the legacy of your family will be strong.

—Dennis & Barbara Rainey

contents

1

What Every
Parent Needs

To be an effective parent, you need to establish a strong foundation for your home.

warm-up

Hello, I'm a Parent

Introduce yourself by telling the group the names and ages of your children and one reason why you decided to join this group.

Next, choose one of the following sentences to complete, and then share it with the group:

- One way my life changed when I became a parent is . . .
- One of the best things about being a parent is . . .
- The longer I'm a parent, the more I appreciate how my own parents . . .
- I didn't realize that when I became a parent, my life would . . .

blueprints

The Challenges of Raising Children

As a parent, it's easy to feel apprehensive and, at times, inadequate. There are no perfect people and no perfect parents. All parents face challenges as they raise their children. Our goal in this study is to provide you with some clear principles and strategies to improve your parenting skills.

1. How would you compare your job as a parent today to what your parents faced? Do you think parenting today is more difficult, less difficult, or about the same? Explain your answer.

2. How does the strength or weakness of your marriage commitment affect the well-being of your children?

3. In what ways does a family benefit when both parents are involved and in agreement in the parenting process? Give an example of a situation when you've seen this in action.

homebuilders principle: You and your spouse need a fresh commitment to your marriage and to a united approach to raising your children.

The Need to Value Children

4. Read Psalm 127:3–5 and Luke 18:15–17. What do these passages tell us about God's view of children?

5. Why do you think it's important to acknowledge that each child is a gift from God? How does this belief influence the way you carry out your responsibilities as a parent?

6. In what specific ways have your children been gifts or blessings for you? What's rewarding to you as a parent?

homebuilders principle: Each child is a divinely placed gift, a high and holy privilege given to parents.

The Need for Convictions

One of the most important things we can do as parents is to establish a set of convictions and ideals to live by. Author Josh McDowell writes that having a conviction "is being so thoroughly convinced that something is absolutely true that you take a stand for it regardless of the consequences." These convictions, or "core values," guide our daily choices and help us establish priorities. They are also the values we pass on to our children. For example, the adage "A job worth doing is worth doing right" is actually a reflection of multiple convictions: the values of working hard, taking responsibility, and striving for excellence.

7. As you think about your mother and father (or the person who raised you), what really mattered to them? What convictions or values would you say governed their lives? What core values did they pass on to you?

8. On the scale that follows, where would you rate yourself on establishing a personal set of core values or convictions?

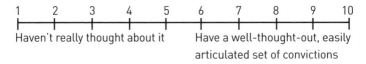

Haven't really thought about it   Have a well-thought-out, easily articulated set of convictions

- List a couple of your convictions:

9. Read Matthew 7:24–27. According to this passage, what's the difference between the wise man and the foolish man? How would you apply this to the process of determining your core values?

homebuilders principle: As a parent, you need to establish core values and base them on the unchanging truth of God's Word.

make a date

Set a time for you and your spouse to complete the HomeBuilders project together before the next group meeting. You will be asked at the next session to share an insight or experience from the project.

date _____ time _____

location _____

homebuilders project

On Your Own

Answer the following questions:

1. What key insight did you gain from this session?

2. What specific steps can you and your spouse take to develop a more united approach to parenting?

3. In the space that follows, or on a separate sheet of paper if needed, take about ten minutes to list as many values as you can think of that you would like to pass on to your children. This is brainstorming time; focus on writing as many convictions as come to mind, and try to keep your statements to one sentence. To help you get started, see the list of "Core Values Possibilities" on pages 9–13.

4. Working from the list you just created, select five core values to designate as your top values and record them here:

    1.

    2.

    3.

    4.

    5.

5. Reflect on your lifestyle and how you spend your time. How well does your life reflect the top core values you selected? Be specific.

With Your Spouse

1. Share your responses to the questions you answered on your own.

2. Talk about the top core values you selected. How similar or different are your lists? Do you agree or disagree with each other's selections? Create a combined "Top-Ten Core Values" list.

1.
2.
3.
4.
5.
6.
7.
8.
9.
10.

3. Discuss specific ways you can teach and model these values to your children. You might want to schedule a series of family nights to address your top-ten values with them.

4. Close in prayer, asking God for wisdom as you seek to model and communicate your core values to your children.

Be sure to check out the related Parent-Child Interactions beginning on page 81.

Core Values Possibilities

While not exhaustive, the following list includes more than fifty topics in eight categories to help spark your thinking.

Spiritual Values

Values under this category might address such topics as

- a personal relationship with God through Christ
- a childlike faith
- a biblical worldview
- an implicit trust in the Bible
- a contrite and tender heart
- an attitude of humble prayer
- a hunger for righteousness
- a healthy fear and reverence for God
- a radical dependence on God
- a forgiving spirit
- a spirit of hope
- a deep and abiding love for God and others
- a submissive attitude toward God and God-appointed authorities

Relational Values

Values under this category might deal with such attitudes as

- respect
- friendliness
- compassion
- grace
- mercy
- care

- thoughtfulness
- kindness
- helpfulness
- generosity

Moral Values

Values under this category might address such topics as

- what you base your moral choices on
- where you stand on specific issues

Civic and Cultural Values

Values under this category might address such topics as

- abiding by the law
- social mindedness
- patriotism

Lifestyle Values

Values under this category might address such topics as

- how you spend your time each day
- how much you emphasize material things
- how strong your work ethic is
- how much you emphasize relationships

Family Values

Values under this category might address such topics as

- commitment to your spouse
- commitment to one another as a family
- importance of grandparents and relatives

Personal Development Values

Values under this category might address such topics as

- personal-health convictions
- intellectual growth
- skill and hobby development
- cleanliness
- discipline

Character Values

Values under this category might address such traits as

- honesty
- lovingkindness
- truthfulness
- faithfulness
- trustworthiness
- obedience
- teachability
- tolerance

- temperance
- patience
- loyalty
- moral purity
- financial integrity

2 Building a Relationship with Your Children

Your success as a parent hinges on developing a positive relationship with your children.

Memory Makers

Building a relationship with your children involves making memories. Pick one of the following questions to answer and share with the group:

- If you could choose one favorite childhood memory of something you did with a parent, what would it be and why?
- What's a favorite memory of an activity you have enjoyed with your own children?
- Why is it important to build shared memories with your children?

Project Report

If you completed the HomeBuilders project from the first session, share one thing you learned.

In this session we'll look at the type of relationship you need with your children to become a more effective parent.

Expressing Love in Your Relationship

A positive relationship with your children is grounded in their knowledge that you love them unconditionally.

1. Practically speaking, what are some ways you can demonstrate unconditional love to your children when

   • they disobey you?

   • they don't meet a performance expectation you have clearly set for them (such as cleaning their rooms or completing chores)?

2. Why is it important to show affection to your children regardless of their ages?

Building a Relationship Requires Involvement

3. One of the best places in the Bible to read about the responsibilities of a parent is in the book of Proverbs. Looking at the passages that follow, how would you describe the relationship between the father and son? In what ways is the father involved in his son's life?

- Proverbs 1:8–10

- Proverbs 3:1–7

- Proverbs 4:1–4

4. What are some of the pressures we face as parents that can make it difficult for us to be vitally involved in teaching, training, and guiding our children?

5. Many parents are very involved in the lives of their children when they are young, but that involvement often decreases as the children approach and enter adolescence. Why do you think this is? Why is continued involvement important?

homebuilders principle: Building a relationship with your children requires a commitment to being vitally involved in teaching, training, and guiding them in God's ways.

Relationship Skills

6. Read Proverbs 12:25 and Ephesians 4:29. In what ways can a parent's praise benefit a child? Is praise easy or difficult for you to give? Why?

homebuilders principle: One of your children's greatest needs is your praise and approval.

7. Read Ephesians 6:4. In what ways might parents exasperate their children? What effect does conflict between you and your child have on the atmosphere in your home?

8. Read Ephesians 4:32. What principles in this verse are important to model to your children? In what practical ways can these principles be modeled?

Rules and Relationship in Balance

Children come into the world with the need for both love and guidance.

9. What can happen in a home when

- a parent emphasizes rules and discipline for a child without a warm and loving relationship?

- a parent emphasizes a loving relationship with a child but is light on rules and discipline?

Parting Thought

Just as God pursues a relationship with us, we should love our children and pursue a relationship with them. This relationship is like a bridge to an island. The bridge allows traffic to flow in both directions—it allows us to love and encourage our children while training them and building their character. Don't let the bridge fall down.

make a date

Set a time for you and your spouse to complete the HomeBuilders project together before the next group meeting. You will be asked at the next session to share an insight or experience from the project.

date _____ time _____

location _____

homebuilders project

On Your Own

1. What one thought from this session challenged you most?

2. What did your mother and father do best as they raised you? (If you were raised primarily by someone other than your parents, answer this question with that person in mind.)

Mom	Dad

3. What could your parents have done better?

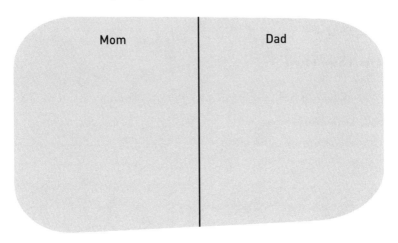

4. What words best describe your relationship with each of your parents?

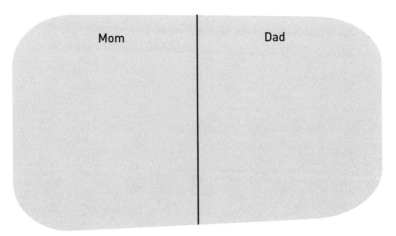

5. Reread Psalm 127:3–5. In what ways have your children blessed your life?

6. How well do you think you have truly received your children as gifts from God—accepting them as they are?

7. Evaluate your relationship with each of your children individually. What do you consider your top two strengths and needs in each relationship? What do your children need from you?

	Child	Child	Child
Needs	1. 2.	1. 2.	1. 2.
Strengths	1. 2.	1. 2.	1. 2.

With Your Spouse

1. Discuss your responses to the questions you answered on your own.

2. A good measure of a relationship is how much you know about another person. To evaluate how you're doing in your relationship with your children, answer the following questions. (Answer these questions individually and then compare your responses with your spouse's.) If you have more than one child, record an answer for each of your children.

   - What's your child's favorite song or music group?

   - What favorite subject has your child recently studied in school or church?

   - What's your child's favorite game?

   - Who's your child's best friend?

   - What's your child's favorite food?

   - What's your child's favorite book or movie?

   To see how you did, plan to ask your children these questions later. For now, compare your answers with your spouse's and then discuss these questions:

- How confident are you that you answered most of the questions correctly?

- How close or in touch do you feel with your children right now?

3. Decide on two action steps that you would like to begin implementing to improve your relationship with each of your children.

Action Steps	Child	Child	Child
	1.	1.	1.
	2.	2.	2.

4. What one memory would you like to make with your child during the next two weeks to build your relationship?

5. Close in prayer, with each of you completing this sentence:

"Dear God, my prayer for my relationship with my children is . . ."

Be sure to check out the related Parent-Child Interactions beginning on page 81.

3

Dealing with Busyness

The closer you look at your family's schedule, the more you'll realize how it reflects your values and convictions.

warm-up

Case Study

Read the following anecdote aloud and answer the questions below:

> Lindsey is a twelve-year-old who has competed in gymnastics since she was six. She has steadily improved, and now her coach wants to move her on to an elite team. She would be required to attend workout sessions three days a week from 4:00 to 8:00 p.m., and she would travel out of town for several weekend competitions.
>
> Her parents, Greg and Lynn, are concerned about the impact this schedule would have on Lindsey and their

family. On one hand, Lindsey loves gymnastics, and they feel an obligation to help her be as good as she can be. It would help build her character. Perhaps, Greg thinks, she might even earn a college scholarship if she keeps improving.

On the other hand, Lindsey has trouble keeping up with her homework and often has to stay up later than her parents prefer. They also have three other children with busy schedules. Their oldest daughter is only a year away from leaving home for college, and Greg and Lynn want to preserve as much family time as possible.

• What options do Greg and Lynn have in this situation?

• What would you suggest they do?

Project Report

Share one thing you learned from the HomeBuilders project from the previous session.

Are You Overloaded?

People throughout history have undoubtedly complained about their busy schedules. But today we have so much more competing for our time, our dollars, and our attention—more options, more choices, more entertainment, more noise, more information, more ministry, more volunteer opportunities . . . more of everything!

1. From the following list, what would you say are the top three factors that have the greatest impact on your schedule?

   - overcommitment
   - job demands
   - church involvement
   - caring for children
   - financial pressures
   - unexpected problems
   - volunteer responsibilities
   - children's extracurricular activities
   - health problems
   - caring for parents or in-laws
   - demands and expectations of extended family
   - my own unrealistic expectations

- hobbies and personal interests
- media time (news and entertainment)
- seasonal factors (holidays, school breaks)
- other: _____
- other: _____

2. How does your typical weekly schedule—and that of your children—affect you emotionally and physically? How do you think it affects your children?

Two Key Questions

In the first session of this study, we talked about the need for parents to develop core values about what is important in life. Dealing with a busy schedule is where the rubber (of our convictions) meets the road (of real life). Why? Because our schedules reflect our values—we devote time to the things that are truly important to us.

To help clarify your convictions and how they relate to your schedule, it's important to ask two questions.

Question No. 1: Why Are We Doing What We're Doing?

3. Why do you think many parents spend so much time taking their children from one activity to the next (sports practices and games, music lessons, dance, and tae kwon do, to name a few)? How can you determine whether you're doing too much?

4. Another activity that takes up more time than we may realize is entertainment. How much extra time would open up in your family's schedule if you instituted a weeklong moratorium in your home on television, movies, music, video and computer games, and the Internet? Does the thought of doing this sound radical to you? Why or why not?

Question No. 2: Above All Else, in What Areas Do We Feel We Need to Succeed?

5. If you were at the end of your life, how would you measure whether you were successful as a parent? In what areas do you feel you need to succeed above all else?

Relieving the Pressure

The Scripture offers practical ways to deal with a busy schedule. Consider the following guidelines.

Use Your Time Wisely

6. Read Ephesians 5:15–17. What do you think "making the best use of the time" means? In what ways have you learned to walk with wisdom and make the best use of your time?

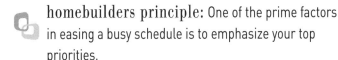 **homebuilders principle:** One of the prime factors in easing a busy schedule is to emphasize your top priorities.

Take Time to Rest

7. Read Exodus 34:21 and Isaiah 58:13–14. Why do you think God placed such importance on a day of rest? If you have applied this commandment in your family, share what you have done and how it has worked.

Deny Selfish Agendas

8. Read Philippians 2:1–4. How can you apply the principles in this passage to the way you use your time?

Make Decisions with Your Spouse About How You Use Your Time

Just after Paul's challenge to the Ephesians to make the most of their time, he exhorted them to submit "to one another out of reverence for Christ" (Ephesians 5:21). One way we've applied this in our marriage is to be accountable to each other with our schedules.

9. What one thing would you be willing to give up to allow more time in your schedule? What do you think your spouse might be willing to give up to make more time?

homebuilders principle: It's important to have regular time with your spouse—such as a weekly date night—to monitor each other's values and priorities as you determine your schedules.

make a date

Set a time for you and your spouse to complete the HomeBuilders project together before the next group meeting. You will be asked at the next session to share an insight or experience from the project.

date _____ time _____

location _____

homebuilders project

On Your Own

1. What did this session reveal to you—good or bad—about
   your family's schedule and priorities?

2. How would you rate the level of busyness for each person
   in your family? List the name of each member of your
   family along with a rating on a scale of 1 (not busy at all)
   to 10 (maxed out).

3. In what ways—positive and negative—are your regularly
   scheduled activities affecting your family? What, if anything, do you need to give up or modify?

4. List the activities each of your children is involved in. Why do you want your children involved in each of these activities?

5. What family activities do you feel are essential to build the atmosphere you desire for your home? What type of weekly interaction do you think is critical for your family?

6. As a family, would you say you have enough time each week to rest and enjoy one another? Why or why not?

7. What changes do you think you should begin making to ensure that your family's schedule reflects the values and priorities you believe are important?

With Your Spouse

1. Review your responses to the questions you answered on your own.

2. Discuss the role of your core convictions in helping you make future decisions about your schedules.

3. Look at your calendars and begin making the necessary adjustments to your daily, weekly, and annual schedules. Talk about what decisions need to be made now so you can begin living according to your priorities.

4. End this time with prayer, asking God for help in making the right decisions about your schedules.

Be sure to check out the related Parent-Child Interactions beginning on page 81.

4

Discipline and Reward

Children need training in how to respond to authority and to the circumstances in their lives.

warm-up

What Would You Do?

With your spouse, choose one of the following scenarios to review. Discuss what you would do in this situation and then tell the group.

Scenario 1: For the first three years after your daughter, Sarah, was born, whenever groceries were needed, either you or your spouse would stay home with Sarah while the other one went to the store. Now you've started taking Sarah with you to the grocery store, and she's been behaving terribly. She grabs food off the shelves and screams when you take it away; when you won't buy candy, she drops onto the floor and throws a tantrum. You're getting ready to take her to the store again.

- How would you handle this situation?

Scenario 2: You've divided a number of household chores among your three children. Your ten-year-old son, Ryan, is responsible for pulling the garbage cans out to the curb each Monday night. For several weeks he did his job, but for the last two weeks, he hasn't. Last week he claimed he forgot, but this morning when you reminded him about his responsibility, he said, "I'm tired of doing all the work. Do I have to do everything around here? Why don't you do it?"

- How would you handle this situation?

Project Report

Share one thing you learned from the HomeBuilders project from the previous session.

blueprints

The Big Picture

As we look at the subject of disciplining children—or more specifically, disciplining and rewarding children—it's important to step back and see the big picture: Setting up a system of discipline and rewards should be part of your plan for building character in your children.

As parents, our job is to build character into our children by training them how to respond to authority and to the challenges they'll face in life. Most parents realize their children require training in everyday living skills—things like tying shoes, cleaning up after themselves, and washing dishes. But children also need training to develop positive character qualities—the ability to choose right from wrong, for example, or to turn away from temptation. As parents, we need to point our children to a relationship with God in which they turn away from their selfish desires and live in obedience to Him.

1. When you think of disciplining your children, what comes to mind?

2. Read Hebrews 12:7–11. What do we learn about discipline from this passage?

3. Since the Bible compares God's discipline to a father's discipline of his children, it's important to note that in addition to disciplining us, God also rewards us for right choices. Read Deuteronomy 30:15–20. What does God promise to those who love Him, obey Him, and keep His commands?

Discipline: A Four-Step Process

Step No. 1: Teach and Set Clear Rules and Boundaries

Parents generally set some common rules and boundaries in the home—to keep children safe, for example, or to make sure the home functions well. But it's also important to set rules and boundaries to develop character traits in each child. For example, if you're training children to be responsible, you might tell them they're required to clean up their rooms a certain number of times each week and then make it clear what will happen if they don't fulfill this responsibility.

4. What are some examples of clear rules or boundaries you could set to teach children of different ages to

- treat other people with respect?

- be honest?

Step No. 2: Praise and Reward Positive Choices

5. Read the verses that follow. If you can, tell the group about something one of your children did recently—made a right choice, did a job well—that's worthy of praise or reward.

- Proverbs 16:24

- Ephesians 4:29

- 1 Thessalonians 5:11

6. What rewards have you used in your household for good behavior? See how many you can list in two minutes. (Write down the ideas from different group members, and use this list as a reference for the future!)

Step No. 3: Correct and Discipline Your Children for Poor Choices

7. Choose one of the following scenarios. What could you do in this situation to correct the child and show how to make a right choice?

   - Your eight-year-old son is playing one Saturday afternoon with a neighbor. Another friend, Jason, phones him and asks him to come over to his house. Your son accepts the invitation and then tells his neighbor, "It's time for you to go home now. I'm going over to Jason's house to play."

- You give your fourteen-year-old daughter a monthly allowance. One week into a new month, she approaches you and asks for more money because she has already spent what you gave her.

8. For some poor choices, children may only require correction from their parents; for other poor choices, children may need discipline. What do the following verses tell us about the benefits of discipline—punishing and reproving children for wrong choices?

  - Proverbs 29:15

  - Proverbs 29:17

9. What forms of discipline have you used and found effective for children of different ages?

A SPECIAL WORD ABOUT SPANKING

Although Scripture makes it clear that spanking can be a useful disciplinary tool, in our culture it's increasingly characterized as cruel and even abusive. Because some parents haven't used this form of discipline wisely, the entire concept of spanking is coming under attack.

We don't believe we should ignore a biblical concept just because some people don't apply it well. But we do recommend that parents agree on some guidelines for spanking:

1. Determine together what attitudes and actions warrant physical discipline. Spanking should not be used indiscriminately; it's just one form of discipline to be used in conjunction with other forms. We've used spanking primarily as a discipline for bad choices that reflect serious character issues—disobedience or lying, for example. We define spanking as a "measured amount of pain" administered to a child to break the will but not the spirit.

2. When you determine your child needs to be spanked, follow these guidelines:
   - Do it promptly, but do it in private, not in public.
   - Only spank when you're in control—not when you're angry.
   - Before spanking, assure the child of your love.
   - When appropriate, explain to the child why he or she is getting a spanking.
   - Use an object that won't harm the child.
   - Hold the child while you do the spanking.
   - Following the spanking, pray for the child and assure him or her once again of your love.

homebuilders principle: Parents must be committed to a balanced training program—rewarding children for good behavior and disciplining them for wrong choices.

Parting Thought

Children will behave like children. That's why Galatians 6:9 is such an encouraging promise: "And let us not grow weary of doing good, for in due season we will reap, if we do not give up." Above all, don't give up!

make a date

Set a time for you and your spouse to complete the HomeBuilders project together before the next group meeting. You will be asked at the next session to share an insight or experience from the project.

date _____ time _____

location _____

homebuilders project

Your goal during this project time will be to develop a plan for how you will use discipline and rewards as you build character in your children.

On Your Own

1. What insight or concept from this session do you most need to apply in your life or home?

2. What is the best or most creative reward you ever received? Why did you get it? What impact did receiving it have on you?

3. Recall a time when you received some form of correction, rebuke, or discipline. Did this have a positive or negative effect on you? Explain.

4. How well do you think you use rewards in raising your children? Explain.

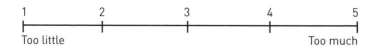

5. Place a check mark next to the rewards you presently use and a plus sign beside any you would like to implement.

___ praise and affirmation

___ hugs and kisses

___ increased privileges

___ bonus allowance

___ a special activity or trip

___ a date

___ a celebration

___ a valued possession

___ an award

___ a special meal

___ other: _____

6. How do you see yourself as a disciplinarian? Explain.

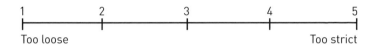

7. What do you most appreciate about the way your spouse disciplines your children?

8. For the following questions, indicate your level of agreement or disagreement.

   My spouse backs me up and doesn't undermine me when I discipline our children.

We are in agreement as a couple about what behaviors we discipline for.

1	2	3	4
Strongly agree	Somewhat agree	Somewhat disagree	Strongly disagree

I back up and don't undermine my spouse when he or she disciplines our children.

1	2	3	4
Strongly agree	Somewhat agree	Somewhat disagree	Strongly disagree

9. Review the following list, placing a check mark next to the top two or three areas you feel the need for improvement when it comes to disciplining your children.

   ___ be more consistent

   ___ raise my voice less

   ___ be more involved

   ___ be more loving

   ___ back up my spouse better

   ___ reward our children more

   ___ be less reactive and more in control

   ___ other: _____

   ___ other: _____

10. Is there a particular discipline problem you need to discuss with your spouse and ask God to help you solve? Explain.

With Your Spouse

1. Discuss your responses to the questions you answered on your own.

2. Agree upon a list of rewards and disciplines you can use to reinforce what you value. Keep in mind that to be effective, a discipline needs to either take away something valued or give something not desired. It must also be age appropriate.

   Keep this list handy so you can refer to it.

Rewards	Disciplines

3. Talk through and list the kinds of offenses that you and your spouse would place in the following categories:

	Major	Moderate	Minor
Younger Children			
Older Children			

Now discuss what type of discipline you feel is appropriate for the different categories of offenses for both younger and older children.

4. Close your time in prayer. Review the items you checked in question 9 of "On Your Own." Pray for each other about these needs.

Be sure to check out the related Parent-Child Interactions beginning on page 81.

5

Becoming a
Better Parent

As a dad or a mom, you need to have a clear
biblical vision of your parenting responsibilities.

Note: For this session, you'll meet in two separate groups—one
for dads and one for moms. The material for dads begins on this
page. Moms, please turn to page 60.

warm-up for dads

Talking About Dad

Discuss these questions:

- When you think of your dad, what words come to mind?
- What important lessons did you learn from your father?

Project Report

Share one thing you learned from last session's HomeBuilders project.

blueprints for dads

Dad as Provider

1. Many of our fathers viewed their first responsibility as being the primary provider for the family. How did your father provide for your family as you grew up?

2. Read 1 Timothy 5:8. Our families need us to provide for them financially, but in what other ways do we provide for them?

Dad as Manager

One of the biggest challenges many fathers face is getting involved in the lives of their families. Many men become passive and let their wives assume nearly all the responsibilities of running the household.

3. Read 1 Timothy 3:4–5. According to this passage, what is one of the key qualifications for someone aspiring to leadership in the church? Why is this qualification so important?

4. When we think of a manager, we often think first of the workplace. What are some characteristics of a good manager in that setting?

5. Using the following chart, contrast an involved father with a passive father in different areas of managing the home. How would the involved or passive father behave in each area?

Involved	Passive
Making decisions about family activities and plans	
Handling and budgeting finances	
Resolving conflict	
Teaching and training children in household responsibilities	
Training children in character development	
Developing and maintaining a system of discipline and rewards	

6. In which of these areas do you feel you need to be more active?

homebuilders principle for dads: You are responsible to God to manage your family well.

Dad as Teacher

7. Looking at the verses that follow, what role does the father in each passage engage in with his children? As a dad, what are some practical ways you have tried to do the same?

   - Proverbs 4:1–5

   - Proverbs 4:10–14

   - Proverbs 4:20–27

homebuilders principle for dads: You are responsible to serve your family as a minister, seeing that your children's needs are met and leading them to seek and serve the Lord.

Dad as Role Model

8. Read Psalm 101. Why is it important to personally model the values in this psalm as you seek to build them into your children?

9. Read Ephesians 6:4. How can failing to model what you teach exasperate or provoke your children? What other actions, or lack of action, on your part could be a source of exasperation for them?

homebuilders principle for dads: You are responsible to be a model of Christ to your family by leading a life of God-honoring character.

warm-up for moms

Talking About Mom

Start this session by discussing these questions:

- What influence did your mother have on the person you are today?
- What did you enjoy doing with your mom? If you could keep just one memory of you and your mother, what would it be and why?

Project Report

Share one thing you learned from last session's HomeBuilders project.

warm-up for moms

Mom as Home Builder

1. In what ways do you feel your upbringing influences your
   feelings and values about your role as a mom?

2. What do the following scriptures tell us about the importance and priority of your role as a mother?

   - Proverbs 14:1

   - Proverbs 31:10–31

   - Titus 2:3–5

homebuilders principle for moms: Motherhood is a gift of God and an opportunity to impact future generations.

Mom as Nurturer

3. As we read in Titus 2:4, older women are told to encourage younger women to love their children. Why do you think this admonition is given?

4. Why do you think a child needs a mother's love so much? How do you as a mother uniquely nurture your children?

5. In what ways can moms show love to their children? For three minutes, brainstorm as many ideas as you can.

6. What do you think are the consequences children face when they're not loved or aren't sure of their mother's unconditional love?

homebuilders principle for moms: You are responsible to love your family so your children can see the love of God in action.

Mom as Trainer

7. Read Proverbs 22:6. How does a mother uniquely train her children?

8. In what areas do your children need training right now?

9. If you feel comfortable sharing, tell the group about an area in which you think you did or are doing a good job of training your children.

homebuilders principle for moms: You are to help prepare the next generation to meet the responsibilities of husband and wife, father and mother.

Parting Thought

One of the greatest needs in our nation is for men and women to stand up and be the fathers and mothers our children need and the Bible instructs us to be. We need to be there when they are young children, teenagers, career singles, married husbands and wives, and parents. Our job and responsibility never end.

make a date

Set a time for you and your spouse to complete the HomeBuilders project together before the next group meeting. You will be asked at the next session to share an insight or experience from the project.

date _____ time _____

location _____

homebuilders project

On Your Own

Note: The first two sections that follow contain three questions for dads and moms to answer separately. Prior to coming back together for discussion, also answer questions 4–6 individually.

Questions for Dads

1. Look back over the material you and the other men discussed during the group session. What points had the most impact on you and why?

2. In the group session, the involved father was contrasted with the passive father. Rate your level of involvement with your children in the following areas:

	Passive/not involved				Actively involved
Making decisions about family activities and plans	1	2	3	4	5
Handling and budgeting finances	1	2	3	4	5
Resolving conflict	1	2	3	4	5
Teaching and training children in household responsibilities	1	2	3	4	5
Training children in character development	1	2	3	4	5
Developing and maintaining a system of discipline and rewards	1	2	3	4	5

3. If you could make just one improvement as a dad, what would that be and why?

Questions for Moms

1. Look back over the material you and the other women discussed during the group session. What points had the most impact on you and why?

2. In the group session, two responsibilities of mothers were discussed: loving their children and training their children. How do you feel you're doing in these areas? Explain.

3. If you could make just one improvement as a mom, what would that be and why?

Questions for Dads and Moms

4. What one thing do you feel you do well in your role as a parent?

5. How can you be more supportive of your spouse in the role of parent? Be specific.

6. What, if anything, do you feel you should be doing as parents that you're not currently doing? Explain your answer.

With Your Spouse

1. Tell each other the main insights you gained during the split-group session.

2. Share with each other your responses to the questions you answered individually.

3. Read Proverbs 22:6. Talk about any specific areas of training your children especially need right now and what you can or should do as a mom or dad to provide this training.

4. Finish your time in prayer, asking God to give you the strength and power to follow through on any commitments you make to become an even more effective father or mother.

Be sure to check out the related Parent-Child Interactions beginning on page 81.

6

Building a Firm Foundation

The most important step to improving your parenting is bringing God into your family.

warm-up

Sand Castles

In session 1 we looked briefly at Matthew 7:24–27, where Jesus talked about the wise and foolish builders. Now let's look at this passage again, following the steps in the exercise below and then discussing the corresponding questions. (Note: You can use this exercise to teach the same lesson to your children.)

For this exercise you'll need

- a rock, approximately the size of a softball
- two or three cups of sand
- a pitcher of water

- a large metal, glass, or foil pan (a nine-by-thirteen-inch
  cake pan or larger)

Step 1: Put the sand in the pan, and then pour a little water over it, just enough to moisten the sand so that you can mold it into shapes. Have one or two people form a small sand castle on one side of the pan. When they're finished, place the rock on the other side of the pan.

Step 2: Read aloud Matthew 7:24–27 and then have someone pour the pitcher of water over the sand castle and the rock. Afterward, discuss these questions:

- What can we learn from this exercise? Write down your observations and then share them with the group.

- Why is a spiritual foundation like the one described in Matthew 7 necessary for your family?

Project Report

Share one thing you learned from last session's HomeBuilders project.

Battling the Storms

1. In Matthew 7:24–27, what do you think the rain, floods, and wind symbolize?

2. What kinds of "storms" have hit your family recently?

3. Do you recall a time when you experienced the truth of this passage—a time when your trust in God and His Word gave you the strength to withstand a storm? If so, share this with the group if you feel comfortable.

4. Different types of storms occur during the different seasons. As you look toward the next few years, what storms do you envision hitting your family?

 homebuilders principle: For your family to withstand the storms of life, you need to build a foundation rooted in God and His Word.

Hearing and Obeying the Word

Over the course of this study, we've discussed many practical principles of parenting that are taken from the Bible. During this time, you've had the opportunity to hear God's Word and apply it to your life. Bible study with life application and prayer are two of the most basic but essential components of a spiritual foundation for your family.

5. Read James 1:22–25. Why do you think both hearing and doing are necessary to build a spiritual foundation in your home? Which is more difficult and why?

6. With your spouse, read the following passages from Christ's Sermon on the Mount:

- Matthew 5:38–46
- Matthew 6:25–34

Then, as a couple, discuss the following questions:

- Think about a time you applied the truth of one of these passages in your family. What was the result?

- What truth from these passages does your family most need to apply right now and why?

If you're comfortable doing so, share with the group your response to one of the previous questions.

Talking with God

God has given us an incredible privilege—the ability to converse with Him. Praying daily with your spouse and children will help you grow closer to God and to one another.

7. With each couple taking one or more of the following scriptures, read the passage with your spouse and discuss what it tells you about prayer. Then report to the group, giving a summary of your passage and your insights.

- Psalm 34:15–18
- Jeremiah 33:3
- Matthew 7:7–11
- Romans 8:26-27
- Philippians 4:6–7
- 1 Thessalonians 5:17
- 1 John 5:14–15

8. How can this group best pray for you? What needs in your life require God's intervention?

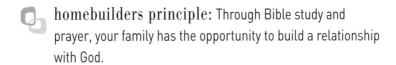

homebuilders principle: Through Bible study and prayer, your family has the opportunity to build a relationship with God.

Building on the Rock

Ultimately, building a strong spiritual foundation for your family depends on you and your relationship with God. God wants a personal relationship with you and has made this relationship possible through Jesus Christ.

You could say that each of us, whether we realize it or not, walks through life on a spiritual journey—a personal quest—to learn what's important and what's true. A quest to find God. Individuals are at different points on this journey:

- Some people have never taken time to seriously consider the truth of Scripture and the claims of Christ.
- Others are seeking for truth and yet haven't come to a decision about whether to commit their lives to Christ.
- Some believe they're Christians but then look closely at their lives and realize that they really don't have a personal relationship with Christ.
- Some have committed their lives to Christ but struggle with a roller-coaster experience; they go through times of walking closely with Christ and times of spiritual dryness.
- Finally, others have made a personal commitment to Christ and are learning to walk in trust and obedience to God.

9. Individually review the following questions and record your responses. Then relate to the group whatever you would like to share.

- On your spiritual journey, where would you say you are? Do any of the descriptions in the previous list apply to you, or would you state them in a different way?

- What impact has your participation in this group had on your view of God and your relationship with Him?

Parting Thought

Many parents reach a point where they realize that something is missing in their family life—a spiritual foundation. They sense a need for God in their family and in their personal lives, but they don't know what to do. Often it takes a storm of life to reveal this need. If you have questions about whether you have personally established a relationship with God, we suggest reading the article "Our Problems, God's Answers" (page 93) and talking to your HomeBuilders leader about what it means to be a Christian.

make a date

Set a time for you and your spouse to complete the HomeBuilders project together.

date _____ time _____

location _____

homebuilders project

On Your Own

1. What was the most important insight or lesson you gleaned from this session?

2. Overall, what insight or lesson from this study has had the most impact on you?

3. Looking back over the study, what intent—something you want to do, stop doing, or change—did you identify? What needs to happen for this to become a reality?

4. What are some of the major storms your family has weathered so far? How have you seen God at work in your family during the hard times?

5. How would you rate your family's past efforts in building a spiritual foundation? On the scale that follows, circle how you would rate yourself individually, draw a box to rate both you and your spouse, and then mark an X to rate your efforts as a family.

	Poor				Good
Prayer	1	2	3	4	5
Bible study	1	2	3	4	5

6. What one thing could you do to improve the rating you gave yourself in the areas of prayer and Bible study? What steps could you take as a couple or family to better practice these spiritual disciplines together?

7. Write down a few thoughts about where you are on your spiritual journey so that you can share them with your spouse.

With Your Spouse

1. Share your responses to the questions you answered on your own.

2. Decide together on two or three action points for strengthening the spiritual foundation of your family. Here are some suggestions:

   - Commit to spending time with God daily in Bible study and prayer.
   - Commit to praying daily with each other.
   - Commit to organizing family devotions every week or two. (If you haven't done the Parent-Child Interactions, that's a great place to start.)

3. Evaluate what you can or should do or continue to do to strengthen your home. You may want to consider continuing the practice of setting aside time for date nights.

4. Spend a few minutes in prayer together. Thank God for each other and for your children. Pray for God's wisdom, direction, and blessing as you continue to seek to improve your parenting and strengthen the spiritual foundation of your family.

Be sure to check out the related Parent-Child Interactions beginning on page 81.

Interaction 1

Family Values

This activity provides the opportunity for you to tell your children about your "core values"—the convictions you and your spouse hold and consider to be the most important. Make sure you complete the HomeBuilders project for session 1 before you begin this interaction with your children.

1. Ask your family: What do you think are some of the values we consider to be most important for us to live by? What things are true, no matter what? (If necessary, provide an example by saying, "For instance: Always tell the truth.")
2. Ask: Where do we get these values from?
3. Say: We believe that a home is only as strong as its foundation. Does anyone know what a foundation of a house is? If anyone is unsure, take the family outside and show them the foundation of your house.
4. Have someone read Matthew 7:24–27. Ask: What does this passage say about what makes a house strong?
5. Say: We believe that a home should be founded on the truth of God's Word. Ultimately, that's what real family values are—truths for living that are based on the Bible.

6. Share a few of the core values that you and your spouse discussed during the session 1 HomeBuilders project. If possible, tell the children what scriptures those values are based on.

Interaction 2

In the Spotlight

In this exercise, you'll direct your family in expressing love and praise for each individual. This is a powerful experience if everyone participates in the right spirit. If you've never done this with your children, it may seem a bit awkward at first. Your children may be hesitant to participate, but with your leadership they'll soon get into the spirit.

1. Call the family together at a time when no one will be hurried. Have someone read Proverbs 12:25 and Ephesians 4:29. Then ask: What do these verses tell us?

2. Explain that you want your home to be a place where people are loved and encouraged. Say: We need to love each other unconditionally, and we need to take time to praise each other for right behavior and attitudes. Sometimes, in the midst of living with each other every day, we don't express this often enough. But tonight each person in the family is going to have a chance to be "in the spotlight" and receive encouragement.

3. Choose someone who will be in the spotlight first. (If you wish, you could use a flashlight and direct the light for a few moments on this family member, making a show

over being in the spotlight.) Say: Each person in the family is going to have the chance to be in the spotlight, and during that time all the others should say at least two things aloud that they like or appreciate about this person. For example, you could say, "I like his sense of humor" or "I appreciate how she always helps me get ready for school each morning." Be prepared to get the family started with some comments of your own.

4. When you finish with one person, move to another. Give everyone the chance to be in the spotlight. When you're done, ask: How did it feel when you were in the spotlight?

Interaction 3

Busy Bodies

This project provides a fun demonstration of what it's like to live a hurried life. Everyone will need a plastic utensil (preferably a knife) and something to balance on the utensil: a coin, bean, button, or potato chip, for example.

1. With your family standing in a circle, follow these steps:

   - Step 1: Find something to balance on your plastic utensil and hold this item steady.
   - Step 2: While still holding your utensil, stand on one foot.
   - Step 3: While holding your utensil and standing on one foot, shake the hand of the person standing closest to you.

2. Then discuss these questions:

- How did you feel trying to accomplish all those things at the same time?
- Are there times when you think you're trying to do too many things?
- Do you feel busyness is a problem in our family? Explain.

3. Read Ephesians 5:15–17. Ask: What do you think it means to make the most of our time?

4. Ask: What should be our top priorities—the most important things to keep doing, no matter what?

5. Ask: If you could change just one thing to make your schedule easier, what would that be?

Interaction 4

You Play the Parent!

Building character involves helping your children learn to make right choices. One of the best ways to teach this is by using hypothetical situations like the ones that follow. These two short scenarios (taken from the group session) give your children the opportunity to examine how to make the right choices and to think about what it's like to be a parent instead of a child.

1. Tell your children the following story: You're an adult with an eight-year-old son. He's playing one Saturday afternoon with a neighbor. Another friend, Jason, phones him and asks him to come over to his house.

Your son accepts the invitation, and then tells his neighbor, "It's time for you to go home now. I'm going over to Jason's house to play."

2. Ask: As the parent, what do you need to tell your son?
3. Instruct a child to read Galatians 5:14. Then ask these questions:

- What does this passage tell us about how we should treat people?
- What do you think it means to "love your neighbor as yourself"?

4. Now read the next story to your children: You've divided a number of household chores among your three children. Your ten-year-old son, Ryan, is responsible for pulling the garbage cans out to the curb each Monday night. For several weeks he did his job, but for the last two weeks, he hasn't. Last week he claimed he forgot, but this morning when you reminded him about his responsibility, he said, "I'm tired of doing all the work. Do I have to do everything around here? Why don't you do it?"
5. Ask: As a parent, what would you do in this situation and why?

Interaction 5

Date Night

Take each of your children out for a date. Don't go on a quick trip for fast food; make this a special day or evening. Take your child to a nicer restaurant, and then go to a movie, a sporting event, a shopping mall, or somewhere else you both would enjoy.

Take this opportunity not only to have fun with your children but also to teach them about manners and about how to treat the opposite sex. If possible, a father should go on a date with his daughter, and a mother should go with her son. To make this special, take the time to call or write an invitation to your child. If you go to a nice restaurant, dress appropriately. If you're a father taking out a daughter, you might give her a flower. And do your best to remember all the manners you've learned over the years: A man opens a door for a woman; a man pulls the chair out for his date and seats her at the table first.

Sometime during the course of the evening, read aloud Romans 12:10: "Love one another with brotherly affection. Outdo one another in showing honor." Then discuss these questions:

- What do you think this verse means?
- How does it apply to the way you treat your brothers or sisters?
- How does it apply to the way a husband and wife should treat each other?
- How do you think this applies to relationships between both boys and girls and men and women?

Interaction 6

Sand Castles

Be sure to complete the other five interactions before doing this one.

For this exercise you'll need

- a rock, approximately the size of a softball,
- two or three cups of sand,
- a pitcher of water, and
- a large metal, glass, or foil pan (a nine-by-thirteen-inch cake pan or larger).

1. Divide the following responsibilities among your children, so they can all be involved:

   - Put the sand in the pan.
   - Pour a little water into the pan—just enough to moisten the sand so that it can be molded into shapes.
   - Form a small sand castle on one side of the pan.
   - Place the rock on the other side of the pan.

2. Tell one of your children to read aloud Matthew 7:24–27. Then have someone pour the pitcher of water over the sand castle and the rock.

3. Then discuss these questions:

   - What can we learn from this exercise?
   - What's the difference between the foundations that the wise man and the foolish man built?
   - What have we learned over the course of these interactions during the last few weeks about how the Bible helps make each of us stronger?

where do you go from here?

We hope that you have benefited from this study in the Home-Builders Parenting Series® and that your marriage and family will continue to grow as you submit to Jesus Christ and build according to His blueprints. We also hope that you will reach out to strengthen other marriages in your local church and community. Your influence is needed.

A favorite World War II story illustrates this point clearly.

The year was 1940. The French army had just collapsed under Hitler's onslaught. The Dutch had folded, overwhelmed by the Nazi regime. The Belgians had surrendered. And the British army was trapped on the coast of France in the channel port of Dunkirk.

Two hundred twenty thousand of Britain's finest young men seemed doomed to die, turning the English Channel red with their blood. The Fuehrer's troops, only miles away in the hills of France, didn't realize how close to victory they actually were.

Any attempt at rescue seemed futile in the time remaining. A thin British navy—the professionals—told King George VI that they could save 17,000 troops at best. The House of Commons was warned to prepare for "hard and heavy tidings."

Politicians were paralyzed. The king was powerless. And the Allies could only watch as spectators from a distance. Then as the doom of the British army seemed imminent, a strange fleet appeared on the horizon of the English Channel—the wildest assortment of boats perhaps ever assembled in history. Trawlers, tugs, scows, fishing sloops, lifeboats, pleasure craft, smacks and coasters, sailboats, even the London fire-brigade flotilla. Ships manned by civilian volunteers—English fathers joining in the rescue of Britain's exhausted, bleeding sons.

William Manchester writes in his epic novel *The Last Lion* that what happened in 1940 at Dunkirk seems like a miracle. Not only were most of the British soldiers rescued but 118,000 other Allied troops as well.

Today the Christian home is much like those troops at Dunkirk—pressured, trapped, demoralized, and in need of help. The Christian community may be much like England—waiting for professionals to step in and save the family. But the problem is much too large for them to solve alone.

We need an all-out effort by men and women "sailing" to rescue the exhausted and wounded families. We need an outreach effort by common couples with faith in an uncommon God. For too long, married couples within the church have abdicated to those in full-time vocational ministry the privilege and responsibility of influencing others.

We challenge you to invest your lives in others, to join in the rescue. You and other couples around the world can team together to build thousands of marriages and families and, in doing so, continue to strengthen your own.

Be a HomeBuilder

Here are some practical ways you can make a difference in families today:

- Gather a group of four to seven couples and lead them through this HomeBuilders study. Consider challenging others in your church or community to form additional HomeBuilders groups.
- Commit to continue building families and marriages by doing another small-group study in the HomeBuilders Parenting Series® or the HomeBuilders Couples Series®.
- Consider using the *JESUS* film as an outreach. For more information contact FamilyLife at the number or website below.
- Host a dinner party. Invite families from your neighborhood to your home, and as a couple share your faith in Christ.
- If you have attended FamilyLife's Weekend to Remember® getaway, consider offering to assist your pastor in counseling engaged couples, using the material you received.

For more information about these ministry opportunities, contact your local church or

FamilyLife
PO Box 7111
Little Rock, AR 72223
1-800-FL-TODAY
FamilyLife.com

our problems, God's answers

Every couple has to deal with problems in marriage—communication problems, money problems, difficulties with sexual intimacy, and more. Learning how to handle these issues is important to cultivating a strong and loving relationship.

The Big Problem

One basic problem is at the heart of every other problem in marriage, and it's too big for any person to deal with on his or her own. The problem is separation from God. If you want to experience life and marriage the way they were designed to be, you need a vital relationship with the God who created you.

But sin separates us from God. Some try to deal with sin by working hard to become better people. They may read books on how to control anger, or they may resolve to stop cheating on their taxes, but in their hearts they know—we all know—that the sin problem runs much deeper than bad habits and will take more than our best behavior to overcome it. In reality, we have rebelled against God. We have ignored Him and have decided to run our lives in a way that makes sense to us, thinking that our ideas and plans are better than His.

For all have sinned and fall short of the glory of God. (Romans 3:23)

What does it mean to "fall short of the glory of God"? It means that none of us has trusted and treasured God the way we should. We have sought to satisfy ourselves with other things and have treated them as more valuable than God. We have gone our own way. According to the Bible, we have to pay a penalty for our sin. We cannot simply do things the way we choose and hope it will be okay with God. Following our own plans leads to our destruction.

> There is a way that seems right to a man, but its end is the way to death. (Proverbs 14:12)

> For the wages of sin is death. (Romans 6:23)

The penalty for sin is that we are separated from God's love. God is holy, and we are sinful. No matter how hard we try, we cannot come up with some plan, like living a good life or even trying to do what the Bible says, and hope that we can avoid the penalty.

God's Solution to Sin

Thankfully, God has a way to solve our dilemma. He became a man through the person of Jesus Christ. Jesus lived a holy life in perfect obedience to God's plan. He also willingly died on a cross to pay our penalty for sin. Then He proved that He is more powerful than sin or death by rising from the dead. He alone has the power to overrule the penalty for our sin.

> Jesus said to him, "I am the way, and the truth, and the life. No one comes to the Father except through me." (John 14:6)

But God shows his love for us in that while we were
still sinners, Christ died for us. (Romans 5:8)

For the wages of sin is death, but the free gift of
God is eternal life in Christ Jesus our Lord. (Romans
6:23)

The death and resurrection of Jesus have fixed our sin problem. He has bridged the gap between God and us. He is calling us
to come to Him and to give up our flawed plans for running our
lives. He wants us to trust God and His plan.

Accepting God's Solution

If you recognize that you are separated from God, He is calling
you to confess your sins. All of us have made messes of our lives
because we have stubbornly preferred our ideas and plans to His.
As a result, we deserve to be cut off from God's love and His care
for us. But God has promised that if we will acknowledge that we
have rebelled against His plan, He will forgive us and will fix our
sin problem.

But to all who did receive him, who believed in his
name, he gave the right to become children of God.
(John 1:12)

For by grace you have been saved through faith. And
this is not your own doing; it is the gift of God, not a
result of works, so that no one may boast. (Ephesians
2:8–9)

When the Bible talks about receiving Christ, it means we acknowledge that we are sinners and that we can't fix the problem ourselves. It means we turn away from our sin. And it means we trust Christ to forgive our sins and to make us the kind of people He wants us to be. It's not enough to intellectually believe that Christ is the Son of God. We must trust in Him and His plan for our lives by faith, as an act of the will.

Are things right between you and God, with Him and His plan at the center of your life? Or is life spinning out of control as you seek to make your own way?

If you have been trying to make your own way, you can decide today to change. You can turn to Christ and allow Him to transform your life. All you need to do is talk to Him and tell Him what is stirring in your mind and in your heart. If you've never done this, consider taking the steps listed here:

- Do you agree that you need God? Tell God.
- Have you made a mess of your life by following your own plan? Tell God.
- Do you want God to forgive you? Tell God.
- Do you believe that Jesus' death on the cross and His resurrection from the dead gave Him the power to fix your sin problem and to grant you the free gift of eternal life? Tell God.
- Are you ready to acknowledge that God's plan for your life is better than any plan you could come up with? Tell God.
- Do you agree that God has the right to be the Lord and Master of your life? Tell God.

Seek the LORD while he may be found; call upon him while he is near. (Isaiah 55:6)

Here is a suggested prayer:

Lord Jesus, I need You. Thank You for dying on the cross for my sins. I receive You as my Savior and Lord. Thank You for forgiving my sins and giving me eternal life. Make me the kind of person You want me to be.

The Christian Life

For the person who is a follower of Christ—a Christian—the penalty for sin is paid in full. But the effect of sin continues throughout our lives.

If we say we have no sin, we deceive ourselves, and the truth is not in us. (1 John 1:8)

For I do not do the good I want, but the evil I do not want is what I keep on doing. (Romans 7:19)

The effects of sin carry over into our marriages as well. Even Christians struggle to maintain solid, God-honoring marriages. Most couples eventually realize they can't do it on their own. But with God's help, they can succeed. To learn more, read the extended version of this article at FamilyLife.com/Resources.

leader's notes

What is the leader's job?

Your role is more of a facilitator than a teacher. A teacher usually does most of the talking and instructing whereas a facilitator encourages people to think and to discover what Scripture says. You should help group members feel comfortable and keep things moving forward.

Is there a structure to the sessions?

Yes, each session is composed of the following categories:

Warm-Up (5–10 minutes): The purpose of Warm-Up is to help people unwind from a busy day and get to know one another better. Typically the Warm-Up starts with an exercise that is fun but also introduces the topic of the session.

Blueprints (45–50 minutes): This is the heart of the study when people answer questions related to the topic of study and look to God's Word for understanding. Some of the questions are to be discussed between spouses and others with the whole group.

HomeBuilders Project (60 minutes): This project is the unique application that couples will work on between the group meetings. Each HomeBuilders project contains two sections: (1) On your own—questions for husbands and wives to answer individually and (2) With your spouse—an opportunity for couples to share their answers with each other and to make application in their lives.

What is the best setting and time schedule for this study?

This study is designed as a small-group, home Bible study. However, it can be adapted for more structured settings like a Sunday school class. Here are some suggestions for using this study in various settings:

In a small group

To create a friendly and comfortable atmosphere, we recommend you do this study in a home setting. In many cases the couple that leads the study also serves as host, but sometimes involving another couple as host is a good idea. Choose the option you believe will work best for your group, taking into account factors such as the number of couples participating and the location.

Each session is designed as a sixty-minute study, but we recommend a ninety-minute block of time to allow for more relaxed conversation and refreshments. Be sure to keep in mind one of the cardinal rules of a small group: good groups start *and* end on time. People's time is valuable, and your group will appreciate your respecting this.

In a Sunday school class

If you want to use the study in a class setting, you need to adapt it in two important ways: (1) You should focus on the content of the Blueprints section of each session. That is the heart of the session. (2) Many Sunday school classes use a teacher format instead of a small-group format. If this study is used in a class setting, the class should adapt to a small-group dynamic. This will involve an interactive, discussion-based format and may also require a class to break into multiple smaller groups.

What is the best size group?

We recommend from four to seven couples (including you and your spouse). If more people are interested than you can accommodate, consider asking someone to lead a second group. If you have a large group, you may find it beneficial to break into smaller subgroups on occasion. This helps you cover the material in a timely fashion and allows for optimum interaction and participation within the group.

What about refreshments?

Many groups choose to serve refreshments, which helps create an environment of fellowship. If you plan to include refreshments, here are a couple of suggestions: (1) For the first session (or two) you should provide the refreshments. Then involve the group by having people sign up to bring them on later dates. (2) Consider starting your group with a short time of informal fellowship and refreshments (15–20 minutes). Then move into the study. If couples are late, they miss only the food and don't disrupt the study. You may also want to have refreshments available again at the end of your meeting to encourage fellowship. But remember to respect the group members' time by ending the session on schedule and allowing anyone who needs to leave to do so gracefully.

What about child care?

Groups handle this differently, depending on their needs. Here are a couple of options you may want to consider:

- Have people be responsible for making their own arrangements.
- As a group, hire someone to provide child care, and have all the children watched in one location.

What about prayer?

An important part of a small group is prayer. However, as the leader, you need to be sensitive to people's comfort level with praying in front of others. Never call on people to pray aloud unless you know they are comfortable doing this. You can take creative approaches, such as modeling prayer, calling for volunteers, and letting people state their prayers in the form of finishing a sentence. A helpful tool in a group is a prayer list. You should lead the prayer time, but allow another couple to create, update, and distribute prayer lists as their ministry to the group.

Find additional help and suggestions for leading your Home-Builders group at FamilyLife.com/Resources.

about the leader's notes

The sessions in this study can be easily led without a lot of preparation time. However, accompanying Leader's Notes have been provided to assist you when needed. The categories within the Leader's Notes are as follows:

Objectives

The Objectives focus on the issues that will be presented in each session.

Notes and Tips

This section provides general ideas, helps, and suggestions about the session. You may want to create a checklist of things to include in each session.

Blueprints Commentary

This section contains notes that relate to the Blueprints questions. Not all Blueprints questions will have accompanying commentary notes. The number of the commentary note corresponds to the number of the question it relates to. (For example, the Leader's Notes, session 1, number 5 in the Blueprints Commentary section relates back to session 1, Blueprints, question 5.)

session one

what every parent needs

Objectives

To be an effective parent, you need to establish a strong foundation for your home.

In this session, parents will

- enjoy getting to know one another,
- examine different ways our changing culture has put extra pressure on today's parents, and
- discuss their need to develop convictions, embrace the value of children, and commit themselves to a team approach to parenting.

Notes and Tips

1. Welcome to the first session of the HomeBuilders study *Improving Your Parenting*. Although it's anticipated that most of the participants will be couples with children, be aware that you may have single parents, future parents, or even one parent from a marriage participating. Welcome everyone warmly and work to create a supportive and encouraging environment.

   You'll find certain features throughout this study that are specifically geared toward couples, such as designated couples questions and the HomeBuilders projects. However, we encourage you as the leader to be flexible and sensitive to your group. For example, if you have a single parent in your group, you might invite that person to join you and your spouse when a couples question is indicated in the study. Or, if there are multiple single parents, you may want to encourage them to join together for these questions. Likewise, for the Home-Builders project at the end of every session, you may want to encourage singles to complete what they can individually or to work with another single parent on the project.

2. If you have not already done so, you'll want to read the information "About Leading a HomeBuilders Group" and "About the Leader's Notes," starting on page 101.

3. As part of the first session, you may want to review with the group some ground rules (see page ix in the introduction).

4. At this first meeting, collect the names, phone numbers, and e-mail addresses of the group members. You may want to make a list that you can copy and distribute to the entire group.

5. Depending on the size of your group, you may spend longer than fifteen minutes on the Warm-Up section. If this happens, try to finish the Blueprints section in thirty to

forty minutes. It's a good idea to mark the questions in Blueprints that you want to be sure to cover. Encourage couples to look at any questions you don't get to during the session when they do the HomeBuilders project.

6. Throughout the sessions in this course, you'll find some questions that are designed for spouses to answer together. The purpose of these questions for couples is to foster communication and unity between spouses and to give couples an opportunity to deal with personal issues. Although couples are free to share their responses to these questions with the group, be sensitive to the fact that not all couples will want to do so.

7. If there is room for more participants, you may want to remind the group that because this study is just under-way, they can still invite another couple to join the group.

8. Before dismissing the group, make a special point to tell couples about the importance of the HomeBuilders project. Encourage them to make a date before the next meeting to complete this session's project. Mention that you'll ask about their experience with the project at the next session.

In addition to the HomeBuilders projects, there are six related Parent-Child Interactions beginning on page 81. These are designed to help give parents an oppor-tunity to communicate with their children. Though we recommend that parents try to complete the interactions between group sessions, we know that this will be a challenge. We encourage couples to place a priority on completing the HomeBuilders projects and then doing the Parent-Child Interactions when they have time, whether between sessions or at a later date.

9. You may want to offer a closing prayer instead of asking others to pray aloud. Many people are uncomfortable praying in front of others, and unless you already know your group well, it may be wise to venture slowly into various methods of prayer. Regardless of how you decide to close, you should serve as a model.

Blueprints Commentary

Here is some additional information about various Blueprints questions. (Note: The numbers below correspond to the Blueprints questions they relate to.) If you share any of these points, be sure to do so in a manner that does not stifle discussion by making you the authority with the "right" answers. Begin your comments by saying things like, "One thing I notice in this passage is . . . ," or "I think another reason for this is . . . ."

2. For one thing, it markedly increases your children's sense of security. If your children know that you're fully committed to your marriage and family, they can focus on growing and maturing rather than worrying about whether Mom and Dad will split up or whether they caused their parents' divorce. Another benefit is that

children learn by the parents' example how to love one another, how to love in spite of difficulties, how to handle conflict, and how to persevere through difficulties.

Potential follow-up questions: Ask if anyone in the group had parents who divorced when he or she was a child. Then ask, "How did this impact you as a child?"

3. Children feel loved and secure. They know there are definite limits to their behavior. They also know they can't cause division by appealing to one parent over the other.

Potential follow-up question: "What can happen in a family when children see that one parent is more involved in their lives than the other?"

4. Children are gifts, a reward from the Lord to be treasured.

5. It should increase our sense of thankfulness, responsibility, and accountability to God as we raise and train our children. It should also push us to seek God's leadership and guidance in the training process. Realizing that we're accountable to God for how we raise our children should make us more aware of our own spiritual growth and accountability to God.

9. In a confusing world where a multitude of differing values are promoted, it's important to base our convictions upon the truth of God's Word.

session two

building a relationship with your children

Objectives

Your success as a parent hinges on developing a positive relationship with your children.

In this session, parents will

- acknowledge the important role that unconditional love plays in forming positive relationships with their children,
- examine the need for parents to be involved with their children and the pressures that often keep them from this involvement,
- discuss the need for parents to praise their children, and
- think about how they can build memories for their families.

Notes and Tips

1. Because this is the second session, your group members have probably warmed up to one another but still may not feel free to be completely open about their relationships. Don't force the issue. Continue to encourage couples to attend and to complete the projects.

2. If new people come this session, during Warm-Up ask them to share the names and ages of their children and why they decided to join the group.

3. If refreshments are planned for this session, make sure arrangements for them have been made.

4. If your group has decided to use a prayer list, make sure this is covered.

5. If you told the group during the first session that you'd be asking them to share something they learned from the first HomeBuilders project, be sure to do so.

6. You may want to ask for a volunteer or two to close the session in prayer. Check ahead of time with a couple of people you think might be comfortable praying aloud.

Blueprints Commentary

1. When your children disobey you, you can show love by controlling your emotions—never venting anger when they disobey you, never disciplining in anger, explaining to them why it's so important for them to learn to obey you and God, and taking time to pray with them before and after any discipline.

When they don't meet a performance standard you've set for them, you can affirm your love for them with your words and a hug. Take time to listen to them, letting them explain their behavior (even if you don't agree with their explanation). And then explain to them why it's important to be responsible and truthful.

2. There's a lot of wisdom in the bumper-sticker question, "Have you hugged your kid today?" Appropriate expressions of affection—both with words and touch—are important tools to use in communicating unconditional love to your children. Younger children need the unconditional acceptance and love communicated by parental affection. Even as children move into the teen years, it's important for mothers to hug their sons and fathers to hug their daughters. When children receive appropriate parental affection and love, they're less likely to be drawn into unhealthy relationships with someone of the opposite sex.

3. The father shows a desire to impart wisdom and discernment to his son and to protect him from the consequences of sin. His involvement is demonstrated by taking the initiative to talk to his son. He knows what his son is facing in the world, so he warns him, begging him to listen to the words of love, experience, and caution. Also, he doesn't appear to adopt a cold, authoritarian tone but instead expresses love and hope.

4. Pressures from work, from other responsibilities, and from personal interests can keep parents from spending adequate time with their children. Attitudes that can hamper their involvement include selfishness, laziness,

feelings of inadequacy, preoccupation with seeking their own happiness and fulfillment, and a willingness to hand over major child-rearing responsibilities to a spouse or to the church.

5. For one thing, it's more difficult to build and maintain a relationship with children as they approach and enter adolescence. As a natural part of the maturing process, they begin to "pull away" emotionally—they want to be with friends more, they want more independence, and they don't want to spend as much time with their parents and siblings. When this happens, some parents pull away themselves and fail to put the same effort into raising their children.

   Another problem is the mistaken belief that adolescents are able to begin making their own decisions and don't need parental guidance as much as they once did. This attitude is encouraged by popular media and advertising, which often portray parents as being old-fashioned and restrictive, while teenagers are depicted as being capable of making wise decisions. In addition, some parents may feel awkward guiding their teenage children because of mistakes they made at the same age. In reality, adolescents need parental guidance more than ever as they begin to face and make a number of difficult choices.

6. Children want to please their parents, and their parents' praise is critical to their growth. It's a basic building block for how children view themselves and their world.

Many parents find it easier to criticize their children than to praise them. Part of this is an outgrowth of a parent's role as teacher and trainer; it's often necessary to correct a child when he or she does something wrong. It often takes a conscious effort for parents to begin praising their children for what they do right. If you have a pattern of overreacting and being critical, it will take a lot of prayer and mental discipline to break this habit. One way to start is to look for one thing every day that you can praise in each of your children. Look for attitudes, actions, and little things that are praiseworthy, such as spending time with a younger brother or sister.

7. Parents can exasperate their children by disciplining in anger, not fulfilling a promise, being overly critical, and being too selfish or busy to spend time with them.

9. Rules and discipline without a positive, loving relationship can wound the spirit of the child. A child might come to the place where he or she feels as if "I can never please, be good enough, or do anything right." Eventually this can lead to rebellion and outright rejection of the parents' values.

A loving relationship without discipline can produce permissiveness or a lack of self-discipline in a child. Children may view this approach as a form of rejection, taking the attitude, "My parents don't really care what happens to me." A parent may be a great friend but a terrible mentor.

session three

dealing with busyness

Objectives

The closer you look at your family's schedule, the more you'll realize how it reflects your values and convictions.

In this session, parents will

- recognize the factors that lead to a hurried lifestyle,
- clarify their convictions about priorities, and
- focus on three practical ways to make the most of their time.

Notes and Tips

1. Remember the importance of starting and ending on time.

2. As a role model for the group, you should complete the HomeBuilders project.

3. Congratulations! With the completion of this session, you'll be halfway through this study. It's time for a checkup: How's the group going? What has worked well so far? What things might you consider changing as you approach the remaining sessions?

4. You and your spouse may want to write notes of thanks and encouragement to the couples in your group this week. Thank them for their commitment and contribution, and let them know you're praying for them. (Make a point to pray for them as you write your notes.)

Blueprints Commentary

3. Children do enjoy being involved in these types of activities, but in many cases, the parents are pushing the kids into too much involvement. Parents feel pressure to make sure their children are developing athletically, intellectually, or musically so that they will be "successful." Children also need time to rest, play, and be with their families.

4. We've become so accustomed to entertainment that we can hardly imagine a day without it. We also use entertainment as an escape from responsibility and reality. The thought of abstaining from media entertainment for even a brief period seems radical because, for most of us, it has become an integral part of life.

6. "Making the best use of the time" means seeking God's wisdom about our priorities and choices so that we can accomplish what He has for us.

7. God knows how much we need rest. He gave us the command to observe the Sabbath because of this, and because, if properly observed, it will lead us closer to Him.

8. Philippians 2:1–4 is an appeal to make the needs of others more important than our own needs. At the base of many decisions about time is the natural tendency to do what we desire. If we first deny our own selfish agendas, we can then look for ways to spend our time meeting the needs of our family.

session four

discipline and reward

Objectives

Children need training in how to respond to authority and to the circumstances in their lives.

In this session, parents will

- look at the subject of setting up a system of discipline and rewards as a part of building their children's character,
- work through a four-step process in setting up a plan for disciplining and rewarding their children, and
- discuss real-life scenarios for applying these principles.

Notes and Tips

1. Physical discipline is a controversial subject in our culture. Although this session doesn't closely examine the subject of spanking, it does include the feature "A Special Word About Spanking." You may want to read this feature (page 46) and then invite comments. If there's disagreement, make two points: (1) We should not ignore what Scripture says, even when we don't totally understand it or agree with it, and (2) physical discipline can

be an effective tool for building character in children, as long as it's not abused.

For a more in-depth look at the topic of discipline, the group may have an interest in considering the HomeBuilders Parenting Series® course *Establishing Effective Discipline for Your Children* as a potential future study.

2. By this time, group members should be getting more comfortable with one another. For prayer at the end of this session, you may want to give anyone an opportunity to pray by asking the group to finish a sentence that starts something like this: *"Lord, I want to thank You for _____."* Be sensitive to those who are not comfortable doing this.

3. You may want to make some notes right after the meeting to help evaluate how things went. Ask yourself questions, such as, Did everyone participate? Is there anyone I should make a special effort to follow up with before the next session? Asking yourself questions like these will help you focus.

4. As you look ahead to the next meeting, dads and moms will be in separate groups for most of the session. You'll need a person to lead the group you're not in. Be sure to make arrangements for this in advance. Your spouse may be a good choice for leading the other group.

Blueprints Commentary

1. To some people the word *discipline* has negative connotations—they immediately think of spanking or even physical abuse.

2. This passage compares God's relationship with us to that of a loving father's relationship with his child. It implies that disciplining a child is a normal part of that relationship and that this is a positive thing for a child. Though discipline is filled with sorrow while it's taking place, it yields "the peaceful fruit of righteousness."

session five

becoming a better parent

Note: For session 5, dads and moms meet in separate groups. Leader's Notes for the moms' section begin on page 125.

Objectives for Dads

Dads need to have a clear biblical vision of their parenting responsibilities.

In this session, dads will

- reflect on their experiences with their own fathers,
- expand their view of their responsibilities as fathers, and
- discuss what it means to be a provider, manager, teacher, and role model.

Notes and Tips

1. This is the only session in this study where fathers and mothers are in separate groups. We feel it's important for fathers to consider and discuss their unique responsibilities with other men who face the same challenges.

2. The Warm-Up questions are designed to help dads open up with one another. You might want to tell the men that sometimes it's difficult to talk about our own fathers

because of the experiences we've had with them, but this discussion is necessary if we truly want to become effective fathers ourselves. We don't want our own children to find it difficult to talk about us when they are adults.

Blueprints Commentary

2. Fathers need to provide spiritually for their families by guiding them to a closer knowledge of how to walk with God. They also need to provide emotionally through encouragement, security, and unconditional love. Although we have a responsibility to provide for our families financially, one of the greatest needs is for men to catch a greater vision. As a father, you have an incredible opportunity to help shape the future by shaping the character of your children.

3. The most tangible way to judge a man's fitness for spiritual leadership in the church is by examining his leadership in the home. Too many men become passive at home and allow their wives to manage everything. God wants husbands and fathers to be active, engaged, and responsible for their families.

4. Good managers accept the responsibilities assigned to them. They give time. They gain knowledge and understanding of the people entrusted to them. They delegate responsibilities to others well. They know how to train others.

7. He's taking the roles of leader, teacher, and counselor.

8. Children learn as much by the example they see as they do by our instruction. If our actions and our words don't match, our children will know that our words mean very little.

9. If you have more than one version of the Bible in your group, read Ephesians 6:4 from various translations. Encourage dads to give specific examples for this question.

Objectives for Moms

Moms need to have a clear biblical vision of their parenting responsibilities.

In this session, moms will

- reflect on their experiences with their own mothers,
- reaffirm the priority of their responsibilities as mothers, and
- discuss what it means to be nurturers and trainers of their children.

Notes and Tips

1. This is the only session in this study where fathers and mothers are in separate groups. We feel it's important for mothers to consider and discuss their unique responsibilities with other women who face the same challenges.

2. The Warm-Up questions are designed to help moms open up with one another. You might want to relate that it's sometimes difficult to talk about our own mothers because of the experiences we've had with them, but this discussion is necessary if we truly want to become effective mothers ourselves. We don't want our own children to find it difficult to talk about us when they are adults.

Blueprints Commentary

2. These passages speak of the importance of a mother placing her home at the top of her priority list. This is a special challenge for many women today who work outside the home because of necessity or the desire to pursue a career.

4. Not receiving a mother's love can affect a child's emotional stability and security as he or she grows up.

session six

building a firm foundation

Objectives

The most important step to improving your parenting is bringing God into your family.

In this session, parents will

- examine the spiritual foundations of their families to see if they are firm,
- identify two ways to strengthen their spiritual foundations, and
- reflect on their own spiritual journeys as they discuss their need for a relationship with God.

Notes and Tips

1. As a part of the last session of this course, you may want to consider having a person (or couple) share what the study or group has meant to him or her.

2. Be sure to have the supplies you'll need for the Warm-Up in this session: a rock (approximately softball-size), two or three cups of sand, a pitcher of water, and a large pan (a nine-by-thirteen-inch cake pan or larger).

3. Question 7 in Blueprints calls for couples to look up different scripture passages. This approach allows people to simultaneously examine multiple passages. This saves time and gives group members the chance to learn from one another.

4. In this session, group members are encouraged to talk about their own spiritual journeys. This is a great opportunity for you to discern where people may stand with God. Some individuals may never have understood the gospel and don't know what it means to be a Christian. Others may need a better understanding of what it means to walk with Christ on a daily basis. A group experience like this often leads people to examine their spiritual lives and determine how to know God.

   Be prepared to explain the gospel in the group if it seems appropriate. Or be available to meet with group members to discuss this topic further if they would like. Read through the article "Our Problems, God's Answers" (starting on page 93).

5. Although this HomeBuilders study has great value, people are likely to return to previous patterns of living unless they commit to a plan for carrying on the progress they've made. During this final session of the course, encourage couples to take specific steps beyond this series to continue to build their homes. For example, you may want to challenge couples who have developed the habit of a "date night" during this study to continue

this practice. You may also want to discuss doing another HomeBuilders study.

7. As a part of this session, you may want to devote some time to planning one more meeting—a party to celebrate the completion of this study!

Blueprints Commentary

1. The rain, floods, and wind can symbolize the storms of life: a job change or loss, deaths, sickness, financial difficulties, major disappointments, personal failures, a crisis in the life of a child, and divorce.

5. It's more difficult to live out what we've heard because it goes against our sinful nature. In other words, we want to do things our way or in ways that are pleasing or satisfying to us. James is telling us to do things according to the Word and will of God.

8. You may want to offer a prayer for these requests, have group members pray together in small groups, or have a few minutes of silent prayer. If your group normally has a closing prayer time, make this question a part of that time.

more tools for leaders

Looking for more ways to help people build their marriages and families?

Thank you for your efforts to help people develop their marriages and families using biblical principles. We recognize the influence that one person—or couple—can have on another, and we'd like to help you multiply your ministry.

FamilyLife® is pleased to offer a wide range of resources in various formats. Visit us online at FamilyLife.com, where you will find information about our:

- getaways and events, featuring Weekend to Remember® and The Art of Marriage®, offered in cities throughout the United States;
- multimedia resources for small groups, churches, and community networking;
- interactive products for parents, couples, small-group leaders, and one-to-one mentors; and
- assortment of blogs, forums, and other online connections.

who is familylife?

FamilyLife® is a nonprofit, Christian organization focused on the mission of helping every home become a godly home. Believing that family is the foundation of society, FamilyLife works in more than a hundred countries around the world to build healthier marriages and families through marriage getaways and events, small-group curriculum, *FamilyLife Today*® radio broadcasts, Hope for Orphans® orphan care ministry, the Internet, and a wide range of marriage and family resources.

about the authors

 Dennis Rainey is the president and CEO of FamilyLife (a ministry of Campus Crusade for Christ) and a graduate of Dallas Theological Seminary. For more than thirty-five years, he has been speaking and writing on marriage and family issues. Since 1976, he has overseen the development of FamilyLife's numerous outreaches, including the popular Weekend to Remember® marriage getaway. He is also the daily host of the nationally syndicated radio program *FamilyLife Today*. Barbara is an artist and author. Her books include *Thanksgiving: A Time to Remember, Barbara and Susan's Guide to the Empty Nest,* and *When Christmas Came.* The Raineys have six children and eighteen grandchildren.